# farm friends

## A VISIT TO THE FARM

# hatherleigh

Improve your life. Change your world

Hatherleigh Press is committed to preserving and protecting the natural resources of the earth. Environmentally responsible and sustainable practices are embraced within the company's mission statement.

Visit us at www.hatherleighpress.com and register online for free offers, discounts, special events, and more!

## farm friends

Library of Congress Cataloging-in-Publication Data is available upon request.
ISBN: 978-1-57826-475-9

Printed in the United States
10 9 8 7 6 5 4 3 2 1

*Farming is a profession of hope.*

— *Brian Brett*

Welcome to the farm. Time to meet your friends!

These pigs like to have fun.

These chickens are out for a walk in the sun.

How many sheep can you count?

Goats are very curious.

They also like to play together.

These bunnies love to cuddle.

Farm dogs keep watch over the animals.

This barnyard cat wants to be your friend.

Say hello to this horse!

These ducks are having fun with their friends.

Have you ever heard a rooster crow?

Or a cow go moo?

These baby lambs are at home on the farm.

Mother hen keeps watch over her chicks.

Look at all the piglets!

This calf likes milk as much as you do!

This baby pig has a day of fun ahead!

Baby goats are very curious.

Here's a smile just for you!

Life on the farm is more fun with friends.

These horses plow the fields.

This dog herds the sheep.

Chickens on the farm…

...lay the eggs.

These handsome sheep…

...produce the most beautiful wool.

Busy bees…

...make sweet honey.

Come visit your farm friends again!